SCHOLASTIC
News
Nonfiction Readers

Ants and Other Insects

by
Mary Schulte

Children's Press®
A Division of Scholastic Inc.
New York Toronto London Auckland Sydney
Mexico City New Delhi Hong Kong
Danbury, Connecticut

These content vocabulary word
builders are for grades 1 -2.

Consultant: Kristin Muller
(M.A., Biology)
Lyonsville, New York

Curriculum Specialist: Linda Bullock

Special thanks to Omaha's Henry Doorly Zoo

Photo Credits:

Photographs © 2005: Dembinsky Photo Assoc.: 2, 5 top right, 14, 15 (Randall B. Henne), back cover (Mark J. Thomas); Dwight R. Kuhn Photography: cover center inset, cover left inset, cover background, 1, 4 top, 5 bottom right, 5 top left, 5 bottom left, 10, 12, 13, 17, 19, 23 bottom left, 23 top right; Getty Images/Will Crocker/The Image Bank: 4 bottom right, 7; Peter Arnold Inc./Tom Vezo: 23 top left; Photo Researchers, NY: cover right inset (Darwin Dale), 23 bottom right (Barbara Strnadova), 11 (Larry West); Robert & Linda Mitchell: 4 bottom left, 9; Visuals Unlimited/Dr. Dennis Kunkel: 20, 21.

Book Design: Simonsays Design!

Library of Congress Cataloging-in-Publication Data

Schulte, Mary, 1958-
    Ants and other insects / by Mary Schulte.
        p. cm. — (Scholastic news nonfiction readers)
    Includes bibliographical references (p.   ) and index.
    ISBN 0-516-24935-5 (lib. bdg.)   0-516-24787-5 (pbk.)
    1. Insects—Juvenile literature. I. Title. II. Series.
    QL467.2.S38 2005
    595.7—dc22

                                                    2005002104

1 2 3 4 5 6 7 8 9 10 R 14 13 12 11 10 09 08 07 06 05

CONTENTS

WORD HUNT

Look for these words as you read. They will be in **bold**.

abdomen
(**ab**-duh-muhn)

head
(hed)

insect
(**in**-sekt)

4

antennae

(an-**ten**-ee)

exoskeleton

(eks-oh-**skel**-uht-uhn)

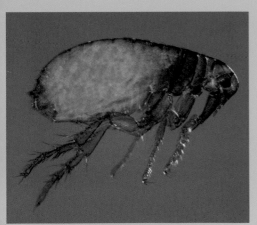

invertebrate

(in-**vur**-tuh-brit)

thorax

(**thor**-aks)

5

 Insects!

Have you ever seen a mosquito, a grasshopper, or a flea?

All of these animals are **insects**.

How can you tell an animal is an insect?

Insects have six legs and three main body parts.

A mosquito is an insect.
How many legs do you see?

Ants are insects.

They have three main body parts.

The first body part is the **head**.

The second body part is the **thorax**.

The third body part is the **abdomen**.

head

thorax

abdomen

9

Ants have two **antennae**.

They are attached to the ant's head.

Ants use their antennae to feel and smell.

antennae

head

This queen ant has wings.

Its wings are attached
to its thorax.

The abdomen holds
the organs.

These organs help break
down the food the ant eats.

wings

wings

13

Insects also have **exoskeletons**.

Some exoskeletons are hard. Some are soft.

Grasshoppers are insects.

They have a hard exoskeleton.

exoskeleton

The exoskeleton helps protect the grasshopper.

Insects are **invertebrates**.

Animals with no backbones are called invertebrates.

Fleas are insects. They have no bones inside at all.

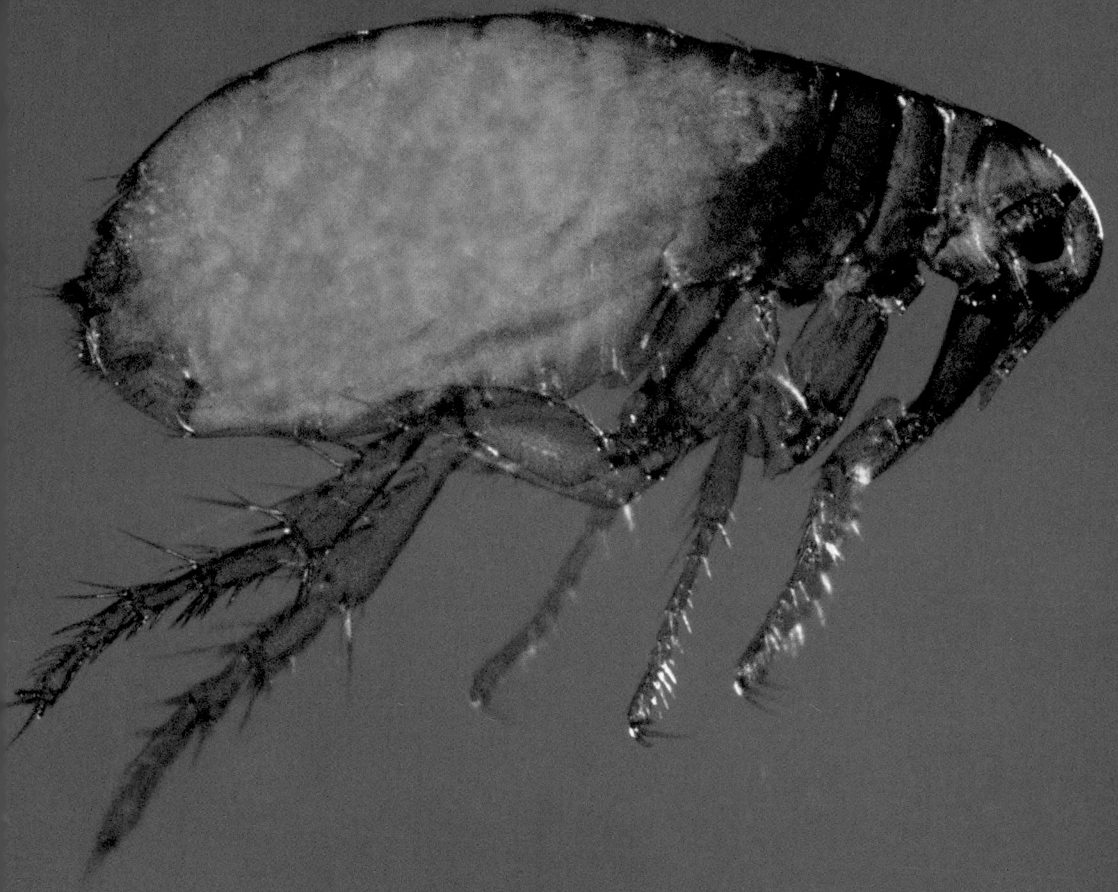

This picture shows the inside of a flea. Can you see any bones?

Some insects are helpful.
They eat pests.

Other insects bother us and carry germs.

Insects are everywhere.

Look around you!

Nobody likes flies on their food. Shoo, fly!

PARTS OF AN INSECT
This Is an Ant.

antenna

eye

antenna

head

thorax

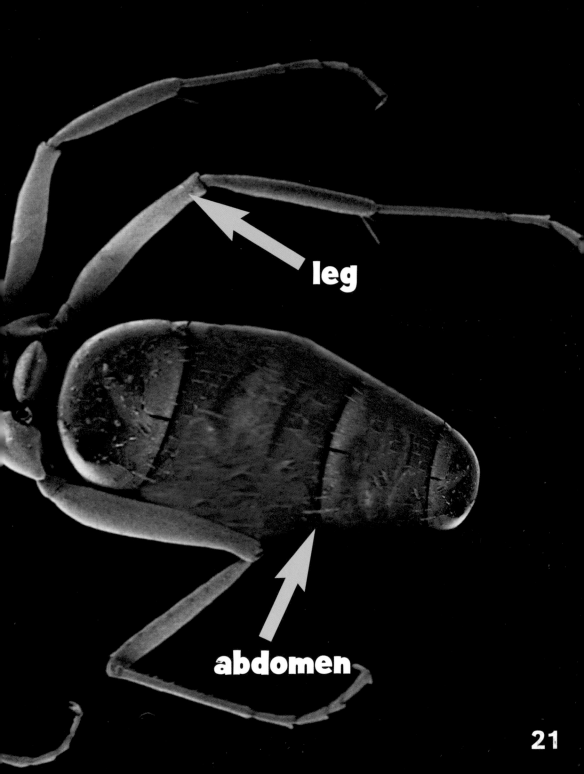

leg

abdomen

YOUR NEW WORDS

abdomen (**ab**-duh-muhn) an insect's organs are inside the abdomen

antennae (an-**ten**-ee) long, thin feelers on an insect's head

exoskeleton (eks-oh-**skel**-uht-uhn) the shell on the outside of an insect

head (hed) the antennae are attached to an insect's head

insect (**in**-sekt) an animal with six legs, three body parts, and an exoskeleton

invertebrate (in-**vur**-tuh-brit) an animal with no backbone

thorax (**thor**-aks) an insect's legs and wings are attached to the thorax

ARE THESE INSECTS?

REMEMBER, INSECTS HAVE SIX LEGS.

centipede

scorpion

snail

spider

23

INDEX

FIND OUT MORE

Book:
The Natural History Museum Animal Closeups: Insects
by Barbara Taylor (Peter Bedrick Books, 2002)

Website:
http://www.enchantedlearning.com/classroom/quiz/insects.shtml

MEET THE AUTHOR:

Mary Schulte is a newspaper photo editor and author of books and articles for children. She is the author of the other Animal Classification books in this series. She lives in Kansas City, Missouri, where there are many busy ants and other insects that visit her backyard.